IMAGES of America
WORLD WAR II SHIPBUILDING
IN DULUTH AND SUPERIOR

On the Cover: The *Dragonfly*, a C1-class cargo ship, was launched on June 16, 1945, and is in the fitting-out stage at the Walter Butler Shipbuilders yard in Superior, Wisconsin. (Courtesy of the Richard I. Bong Veterans Historical Center.)

IMAGES of America
WORLD WAR II SHIPBUILDING IN DULUTH AND SUPERIOR

Gerald Sandvick

ARCADIA
PUBLISHING

Copyright © 2017 by Gerald Sandvick
ISBN 978-1-4671-2581-9

Published by Arcadia Publishing
Charleston, South Carolina

Printed in the United States of America

Library of Congress Control Number: 2016958666

For all general information, please contact Arcadia Publishing:
Telephone 843-853-2070
Fax 843-853-0044
E-mail sales@arcadiapublishing.com
For customer service and orders:
Toll-Free 1-888-313-2665

Visit us on the Internet at www.arcadiapublishing.com

Millions of men and women worked in factories and served in uniform to win the war. This book honors their memory and the memory of a special two: Lucille and Norman Sandvick.

CONTENTS

Acknowledgments		6
Introduction		7
1.	The Warships	11
2.	The Cargo Carriers	27
3.	Shipyards and Workers	45
4.	Tugboats and Auxiliaries	63
5.	Lakers, Tankers, and Cutters	77
6.	Celebrities and Ship Launchings	95
About the Organizations		127

Acknowledgments

No author can assemble a work of history such as this without significant help from others. From Bob Fuhrman, director of the Richard I. Bong Veterans Historical Center, came the initial inspiration and encouragement. My wife, Lynda, must also have my thanks for her ongoing patience and encouragement.

Duluth and Superior are fortunate in having librarians and archivists who are both knowledgeable and eager to help. Those much deserving of my appreciation are Mary Ann Norton, Duluth Public Library; Shana Aue, Jim Dan Hill Library; Mags David, Kathryn A. Martin Library; Teddie Meronek, Superior Public Library; and Briana Fiandt, Richard I. Bong Veterans Historical Center.

The photographs used in this book are from the following sources:

DPL   Duluth Public Library
SPL   Superior Public Library
KML   Kathryn A. Martin Library
BVC   Richard I. Bong Veterans Historical Center
JDH   Jim Dan Hill Library

INTRODUCTION

The Allies prevailed in World War II for many reasons, but preeminent among them was the industrial capacity of the United States. Between 1940 and 1945, the aggregate of airplanes, vehicles, armaments, foodstuffs, clothing, and ships that were turned out was truly astonishing. It has been said that when Hitler challenged the Royal Air Force, he asked for defeat; when he challenged the Russian army, he asked for disaster; but when he challenged the American economy, he was doomed.

In the months after the spring of 1940, Britain stood alone against Germany and needed help that realistically could only come from one place. The British merchant fleet did not have enough ships to handle the nation's import needs and was falling further behind every month as the German submarines took their deadly toll. Shipyards could not build fast enough to stay ahead of U-boat sinkings.

In the fall of 1940, a group called the British Merchant Shipping Mission came to the United States with the express purpose of purchasing cargo vessels. In a fortunate convergence, the United States had been increasing the size of it its own merchant fleet under the Merchant Marine Act of 1936. To accomplish this expansion, existing shipyards were upgraded, new ones built from scratch, and new ship designs developed and standardized for production. The British mission was cordially received and its requests acted on.

On January 3, 1941, President Roosevelt authorized the Emergency Shipbuilding Program, which began placing orders for hundreds of new ships, some to be sent to Britain; and he authorized new shipyards to build them. An existing body, the US Maritime Commission, had its powers increased and was put in charge of all non-naval ship construction.

The United States was still neutral in the European war, but it was the president's firm policy that all necessary aid to England was in the best interest of this country. On December 7, 1941, American neutrality vanished. With the United States now at war with Germany and Japan, many more ships, some to fight and some to haul cargo, were needed.

As war production ramped up in 1942, it was obvious that war across both the Atlantic and the Pacific would be demanding. If tanks and bullets could not be gotten across, they were of no use. Distances in the Pacific were daunting, and U-boats were a major threat in the Atlantic.

Starting in 1941, orders for new ships came to Great Lakes shipyards as well as the coastal yards; indeed, the Great Lakes were called America's fourth coast. Shipbuilding there had two principal limitations: the northern climate that impeded, but did not stop, winter work and access to the ocean. There are two routes to the high seas from the Great Lakes, the St. Lawrence River and the Chicago Ship and Sanitary Canal, which connects Lake Michigan to the Gulf of Mexico through Chicago and the Des Plaines and Illinois Rivers to the Mississippi River.

The modern St. Lawrence Seaway that can accommodate large vessels opened in 1959. World War II vessels were limited to about 250 feet by locks along the Québec sections of the river. The distance from Duluth to the Gulf of St. Lawrence is 2,340 miles. The Chicago route was mostly limited by water depth, primarily the Mississippi River's navigable channel of nine feet. Clearance under bridges was also a factor, but careful planning of a ship's draft and balance made it work. On some vessels, temporary pontoons were welded on to decrease the draft to safe levels. The distance from Duluth to Chicago via Lake Superior and Lake Michigan is 800 miles, and from Chicago to the Gulf of Mexico is 1,530 miles.

These routes limited the size of the ships, and of course, transit through winter ice could be difficult. Still, ships of considerable size could be built, and the Allies needed every vessel they could get. The inland yards also freed space in the coastal shipyards where the battleships, aircraft carriers, and biggest merchant vessels had to be built and war-damaged ships repaired.

Lake Superior is the northernmost and least populated of the five Great Lakes, and the only World War II shipyards were on the far west end, in Port Arthur and Fort William (now Thunder Bay), Ontario, and the Twin Ports of Duluth, Minnesota, and Superior, Wisconsin. In the Twin Ports, about 200 ships were built by five to eight yards, the number depending on the exact date because of closings and mergers. The five principal yards produced several categories of ships, as illustrated in this volume.

The warships were, by definition, armed vessels built for combat. Early in the war, the main threat was interdiction of merchant traffic crossing the Atlantic by German submarines. Fighting the U-boats was a priority, and armed escorts to shepherd merchant convoys were desperately needed in 1941 and 1942.

Subchasers were the smallest antisubmarine vessels in the inventory at 110 feet, and four were built by Inland Waterways of Duluth. Inland was created to acquire a Navy contract for these small ships and built four of them but ran into financial problems and went out of business in 1942. The subchasers were built entirely of wood and were lightly armed but still dangerous. A submarine's defense is stealth, and once found, it is vulnerable to gunfire and depth charges. The mission of these small ships was not to do outright battle but to force the submarines to keep their heads down—to chase them away, as it were. Their weapons were one 3-inch gun, two .50-caliber machine guns, depth charges, and the Mousetrap, a lightweight weapon that fired rocket-propelled bombs ahead of the vessel in a pattern calculated to hit a submerged submarine. They were small but seaworthy and operated in the Mediterranean and the farthest reaches of the Pacific. Few survived the war, and only one survives as of this writing—the *Hitra*, a museum ship in Bergen, Norway, restored to World War II configuration.

Two of the shipyards, Butler and Globe in Superior, built 20 patrol frigates, the largest class of warships built in the Twin Ports. They were originally called corvettes, but that name was soon changed to patrol frigate, and the ships all carried a PF number on the hull. They were conceived as antisubmarine ships and were a modified British design that could be quickly built and put into service. They had more range and firepower than the smaller subchasers and were built for the Maritime Commission, not the Navy. Coast Guard crews manned many of them.

The PFs saw little real action in the war, however, because delays of steel and other basics did not allow them to come into service until 1943. By then, more capable escort vessels had been built and new radar technology and other developments had significantly lessened the U-boat threat. Several Superior-built PFs did have postwar careers as weather reporting ships in the Atlantic and with foreign naval forces.

Cargo ships were the greatest wartime need, and 77 were built by Globe and the two Walter Butler yards. These were 26 N3-class ships and 51 of the larger C1 types with lengths of 259 and 338 feet, respectively. Their relatively shallow draft made them ideal for the mundane but vital task of hauling supplies to American forces on the many Pacific islands taken as the war moved across the Pacific toward Japan. There is sometimes a misconception that the famous Liberty ships were built in Duluth-Superior yards, but at 441 feet long and with a deep draft, they were far too large to have made the transit to the ocean. Only coastal shipyards built them.

Globe Shipbuilding sent 10 large V4 oceangoing tugs off to war. There was a great need for tugs of all sizes to assist the flood of wartime nautical operations. The V4s were among the largest, and three of the Globe-built tugs were direct participants in the D-day landings in northern France in 1944. They may not have been classified as warships, but they did have minimal armament and did come under enemy fire.

Praised by captains and crew for how strong they were, they were built for the Maritime Commission and government-owned but were operated under contract by a private company, Moran Towing of New York. Few tugs of any size survived long after the end of hostilities, because a civilian market for hundreds of surplus tugs did not exist.

Two neighboring shipyards in Duluth, Zenith Dredge and Marine Iron, turned out 38 buoy tenders for the Coast Guard. They were officially called the Cactus and Iris classes but were more commonly known simply as the 180s, because that was the length of the vessels. They were all-purpose ships that did ice breaking and buoy tending and went to war in the Pacific, where they did survey work to improve chart accuracy, installed radio navigation beacons, and did salvage work. Many continued to operate for 50 years after they were launched, vessels so well built they were hard to replace with something better.

Zenith and Marine Iron also built a family of related auxiliary craft for the Navy. The YN types were designated net tenders and water tankers. They had little glamor or dash, but Americans on Pacific islands and elsewhere where freshwater was scarce found them anything but unglamorous. There was always a danger of a submarine attacking ships at anchor or in harbor, and the net tenders' job was to emplace heavy steel nets designed to stop or detonate a torpedo short of its mark. The fact that there was a need for these types of auxiliary vessels speaks to the worldwide nature of the war and the complexity of the logistics of fighting such a war.

The shipyards of the Twin Ports were a major industry during the war and, along with shipping out millions of tons of iron ore, the area's main contribution to the war effort. Labor was in short supply, and the shipyards were always recruiting. Speed and efficiency in production were prized goals, and workers were continuously exhorted to work safely, avoid injury, not be slackers, and avoid idleness and gossip. Competitions between various departments were well publicized, and a department would be well praised if it had the most cumulative days without on-the-job injury.

The majority of yard workers were men, but women, as elsewhere, were a sizable minority, and shipyard work demolished the idea that women could not do hard, dirty, and dangerous work. The shipyard newspapers commonly ran stories about the "welderettes" and breezily reported on how splendid a job "the girls" were doing. Billboards near yard entrances often touted war bond sale records, numbers of days to build a ship, or days amassed with no lost time. The shipyards were the center of wartime activity, and a crowning moment was, of course, the formal launching of a completed ship. The launching ceremonies became theater in which hard work could be recognized, people could be honored, patriotism could be celebrated, and publicity earned. Since a ship sponsor was always female, the wives of governors, members of Congress, mayors, and prominent businessmen were often honored, but celebrity actresses brought the greatest publicity. The Butler firm accomplished a master stroke of publicity in bringing the Dionne quintuplets to Superior in 1943 and launching five ships in one day.

With the end of the war, the Duluth-Superior shipyards quickly wound down their business. There was no demand for new commercial cargo ships when ports were filled with war surplus. Attempts were made to convert to peacetime manufacturing of other products, but the business was not there. The sites of the shipyards were gradually converted to other uses, and years later, only one shipyard would remain on the Superior side of the harbor.

One
THE WARSHIPS

The Duluth-Superior shipyards produced two types of ships designed to fight enemy submarines. They were the wood-hulled 110-foot subchasers and the larger, steel-hulled PFs, or patrol frigates, shown here. USS *Woonsocket* (PF-32) presents a good view of her starboard beam as she cruises Lake Superior just off Duluth in late 1943. A total of 96 Tacoma-class frigates were built during the war at yards on the East and West Coasts as well as on Lakes Erie, Michigan, and Superior. Two shipyards, Globe and Walter Butler, both in Superior, Wisconsin, built a total of 20 of these 304-foot-long frigates. They were lightly armed but had enough firepower to keep enemy submarines at bay. (BVC.)

The SC-670 was one of four 110-foot subchasers built by Inland Waterways of Duluth. A small, family-owned business, Inland received a Navy contract and began building SC-670 a few weeks before Pearl Harbor brought the United States into the war. Craftsmen who knew wooden boat building were hired, and northern Minnesota and Wisconsin had an abundance of raw materials for rapid construction of these vessels. (JDH.)

The heavy oak beam that constitutes the keel of SC-670 has been laid, and construction is under way. The early PC designation, noted on the original photograph, was changed to the SC early in the war. The SCs were built in a large shed on Duluth's Park Point and launched into Superior Bay, a body of water protected from the occasional fury of Lake Superior. (JDH.)

With the building of SC-670 well advanced, the forest of wood scaffolding around the hull is noticeable. Often called "the Splinter Fleet" because of their construction, the SCs were small but seaworthy enough to cross the Atlantic and Pacific. The four Inland subchasers were all launched during 1942. (JDH.)

SC-671 shows her lines and patriotic bunting upon launching on August 8, 1942. The Duluth Coast Guard station is in the background. The small size of the subchaser can be judged by the figures on deck. SC-671 operated in the Pacific from Alaska, Okinawa, Guam, and Kwajalein. She was decommissioned at Pearl Harbor in December 1945. (JDH.)

With a commissioning party on deck, SC-670 began her career in July 1942. Her wartime crew was three officers and 25 enlisted men. They were known as wet ships; they were seaworthy enough, but clothing and bedding was always damp except when hung aloft to dry while in port. (JDH.)

The USS *Poughkeepsie* (PF-26) was launched in August 1943 and shows her full form entering the Duluth Ship Canal after a sea trial on Lake Superior. In 1944, she did antisubmarine and convoy escort duty on the East Coast and was later transferred to the Pacific fleet. In July 1945, she went to Alaska via Seattle to be transferred the Russian navy under the Lend-Lease Act. There, she was then known as *EK-25* for four years until returned to the US Navy. Consigned to the rebuilding Japanese navy in 1953 as a coastal patrol and, later, a training ship, she was finally sold for scrap in 1969. (SPL.)

Work progresses on the USS *Sheboygan* in the spring of 1943. The patrol frigates were built under the auspices of the US Maritime Commission and were officially designated as S2-S2-AQ1 vessels. They had a US Navy service number and were named after smaller US cities. This view of the USS *Sheboygan* (PF-57), with the shipyard workers on and alongside, shows the size of even the small warships. (JDH.)

The USS *Covington*'s construction is well under way in May 1943. The ships were over 300 feet long, and clearly a large quantity of steel plates and girders was required. The United States may have out-produced all other nations in steel, but it still had to be carefully allocated among all the shipyards. (JDH.)

The Globe Shipyard's first patrol frigate was the *Covington*, and rapid construction was a must in wartime. The hulls were welded, not riveted, and it was found that building them upside down allowed the welder to avoid time-consuming overhead welding. The technique was safer and faster and is seen here with welders at work with tanks and hoses evident. (JDH.)

Walter Butler Shipyard was the largest in Duluth and Superior and built 12 patrol frigates. In September 1943, the USS *Grand Rapids* sits on her building blocks, ready for a sideways launch. The silos on the other side of the launch slip are evidence that millions of tons of midwestern grain were shipped out of the Twin Ports. (BVC.)

Once launched, the frigates still had a good deal of fitting out to be done at dockside. In September 1943, the USS *Newport* underwent just such work. Upper deck works were finished, and on the stern, rails to guide dropping antisubmarine depth charges have been completed. (BVC.)

The fitting out, or completion of building after the launch, required much dockside equipment and labor before the ship left the yard. The USS *Emporia* was fitted out in the autumn of 1943. After the war, she was used as weather reporting ship in the North Atlantic. (BVC.)

As was true of her sister ships, the USS *Covington* was powered by two 5,500-horsepower reciprocating steam engines. The boilers were fired with heavy oil that had to be heated before being injected into the firebox. The twin screws, or propellers, gave the PFs good maneuverability. (JDH.)

19

Shortly after launch, the USS *Sheboygan* is tied up dockside. Named after the Wisconsin city on Lake Michigan, she was held in reserve until late in the war and then served as a weather ship based in Newfoundland. In 1947, she was turned over to the French navy, which continued her use as a weather ship. She seems to have been scrapped in the 1960s. (JDH.)

The USS *Shreveport* shows her rakish lines in a spectacular bow-on photograph taken in July 1943. For small ships, the PFs handled rough seas well and were not needed for antisubmarine patrols by 1944, hence their use as weather ships. The *Shreveport* operated out of Newfoundland and, later, Recife, Brazil, for reporting conditions in the South Atlantic. Her career was shorter than most, as she was scrapped in 1947. (SPL.)

Globe Shipyard's USS *Covington* was ready to launch on July 15, 1943. The ship is ready to slide down the ways and, on the platform near the bow, the official launch party and sponsor are ready to christen the ship. Young boys in the foreground and yard workers behind the speaker's platform were common sights, as ship launches were popular events. After the war, the *Covington* was sold to the government of Ecuador and served as the patrol ship *Guayas* until 1975. (JDH.)

The USS *Newport* is pictured on August 15, 1943, ready to go in a dramatic nighttime launch. The banner hanging from the bow is the US Maritime Commission's emblem, a stylized eagle with its wings in a V for victory. The commission's motto was "Ships for Victory." The *Newport* had a varied career, serving in the US Navy as a convoy escort and then being loaned to the Russian navy before being returned to the US Navy. Updated and refurbished, she was thrown into the Korean War in 1950 to guard landings, and in 1952, she was loaned to the Japan Maritime Self-Defense Force. Her employment ended with her 1966 decommission, and she was sold for scrap in 1969. (Right, SPL; below, BVC.)

The USS *Woonsocket* was one of the 12 frigates build by Walter Butler's Superior shipyard. Workers were encouraged to buy war bonds during the frequent national bond drives to help finance the war. The banner reading "Back the Attack" was a part of one such bond drive. The *Woonsocket* also served as a weather ship out of Newfoundland and ended her sailing days as the Peruvian navy's *Galvez* before being scrapped in 1962.

Globe Shipyard's first two patrol frigates were dock mates in mid-October 1943. The second vessel built, *Sheboygan*, is tied up next to the first, *Covington*. Deck machinery is clearly visible, as are the portholes to give the helmsman a forward view. These ships were built to last for the duration of the war, but both served for many years after. October was too early for ice in Superior Bay, but the hillside of Duluth in the distance has an autumn look, and to the right, Duluth's landmark aerial lift bridge can just barely be seen. (BVC.)

The USS *Dearborn* (PF-33) was the last frigate build by the Walter Butler yard and is seen here with sister ship USS *Grand Rapids*. *Dearborn*, like many of her sisters, operated as a weather ship in the North Atlantic, but unlike many, her life was a short one. Commissioned in September 1944, she was laid up in May and decommissioned in June 1946. A year later, she went to the scrapyard. (SPL.)

The USS *Muskegon* (PF-24), named after the Lake Michigan city, is resting on blocks and looking quite ready to hit the water. The hours before launch were a delicate time, as the ship had to be secure but not so secure she would not go down the ways when the last support was knocked out on July 25, 1943. *PF-24* ended her career as a vessel of the French Ministry of Transport. (BVC.)

The USS *Woonsocket* steams out into Lake Superior for trials in the autumn of 1943. The ship is probably working up to full power, as evidenced by the bow wave and the smoke exiting the stack. To the left in this view is Duluth's iconic aerial lift bridge, and on the far right are a warehouse building and twin water towers, both very much still there and recognizable as of this writing. (SPL.)

Two

THE CARGO CARRIERS

Two classes of cargo vessels were built in Twin Ports yards during the war, the Maritime Commission's N3 and the somewhat larger C1 types. The *John D. Whidden*, shown here coming out into Lake Superior, was built in 1944 by the Walter Butler Duluth Shipyard. The Walter Butler Company was a large, well-established construction firm in St. Paul, Minnesota, that operated two shipyards—one in Superior and one in Duluth. The N3 ships were built in both Butler yards; the *Whidden* was one of eight built at the Duluth site. Her service life was 14 years: as an Army freighter, then with the US Navy, where her name was changed to *Aquarius* (AK-263), then loaned to South Korea, and finally sold to ship-breakers in 1960. (JDH.)

The Walter Butler Superior facility had two N3s under assembly in November 1942, the *Anthony Enright* (above) and the *Asa Eldridge* (below). The N3s, at 259 feet long with a beam of 42 feet, may have been classified as small cargo ships, but these photographs show that the construction job was a large and intricate one. The photograph below shows the installation of a forward bulkhead. Many of the workers were newly trained welders, pipefitters, electricians, and others who had never been in a shipyard before. The *Enright* and *Eldridge* were both built to be sent to the Ministry of War Transport for cargo hauling in Britain's war effort. Power came from a 1,300-horsepower reciprocating steam engine. The *Enright* was launched on December 7, 1942, marking the anniversary of Pearl Harbor. (Both, BVC.)

The *Richard Bearse* received the complex of deck machinery in November 1942. The N3s had four cargo holds and deck cranes to hoist cargo in and out of them. Cargo capacity was measured in cubic feet. An N3 could carry enough to fill a warehouse 125 by 125 feet with an 8-foot ceiling. Tonnage was pegged at about 2,200 long tons. (BVC.)

With the remains of the winter's snow in the background, the *Calvin Coggin* is nearing completion in March 1943. She was one of eight N3-S-A1 ships completed specifically for the British. The A1 suffix indicated that her steam engine was fueled with coal, which Britain had in abundance. Other N3s had an *A2* suffix, indicating that the boilers were fired by oil, a commodity that the United States had in abundance. (BVC.)

The *William Bursley*, like her sister N3s, was called a "coastal freighter," and with a draft of under 21 feet, they could get into smaller harbors or in close to Pacific islands. The *Bursley* is seen here in the final stages of her construction in the spring of 1943. Two partially completed sister ships are nearby, and ducks and herring gulls, it may be noted, have found open water amid the late-spring ice. (BVC.)

The *Rodney Baxter*, one of the N3-S-A1 variants built for Britain, can be seen nearing completion in these two photographs, taken in March 1943. The snowdrifts remaining dockside are evidence that the shipyard work was not seasonal and that outside work during Lake Superior's winters was a challenge. The *Baxter* had an adventurous life for a ship planned just for World War II service. With the name changed to *Anguslake* and then to *Dogye*, a gale blew her ashore in South Korea in 1959. Refloated with severe bottom damage, she was towed to Pusan and repaired. Then, in the early 1970s, the ship was sunk by a mine while hauling cargo to Phnom Penh, Cambodia. Raised and repaired, in 1974 she was holed by communist rocket fire and sank in the Mekong River. Clearly, her destiny lay a couple of wars after the one for which she was built. (Both, BVC.)

31

The picture-perfect launch of the *James Miller* came on a fine October day in 1943. A ship always has a sponsor for the launch, and on this day, Mrs. Paul Neilson did the honors. She was the wife of the general superintendent of the Butler Shipyard. The *James Miller* was an N3-S-A2 variant. In Maritime Commission nomenclature, *N3* meant the design of a ship, the *S* signified she was steam powered, and the *A2* meant oil was her fuel. (JDH.)

In 1944 and 1945, Walter Butler yards in both Duluth and Superior and the Globe Shipbuilding Company in Superior had begun building the C1-M-AV1, a larger cargo vessel than the N3s built earlier. The 1945 launch of the *Dragonfly* is beautifully shown in this photograph of the day. The Maritime Commission banner and patriotic bunting proudly decorate the bow as *Dragonfly* makes her first splash, and Duluth and the lift bridge are clearly seen directly across the bay. (BVC.)

The C1-M-AV1 ships were diesel powered—the M in the designation meant motor, as opposed to an S for steam. The C1s were built with an eye toward transportation needs in the Pacific theater of war, where distances meant long voyages and slow turnaround for a round-trip. This photograph, from the Walter Butler Superior yard, shows several workers on deck, most obviously lowering a major engine section into the engine room below. The engine was a 1,750-horsepower diesel from the Nordberg Company of Milwaukee, Wisconsin. Established in 1886 as a maker of steam engines, Nordberg had been manufacturing diesels since 1924 and was a major builder of maritime diesels in World War II. (BVC.)

While the Navy and Maritime Commission orders kept East, West, and Gulf Coast shipyards busy building the larger Liberty ships and troop transports, the Great Lakes shipyards were tasked with building hundreds of vital smaller cargo vessels to take pressure off the coastal yards. The C1 and N3 types were the most numerous of them. The *David R. LeCraw* is seen here in 1944 nearly completed at the Walter Butler fitting out dock in the Riverside area of Duluth. The *LeCraw* was one of 59 N3-S-A2 oil-fueled ships of this group and Butler Duluth built eight of them. (BVC.)

These two photographs of the *John D. Whidden* show the standard layout of the N3 design. It originated with a British purchasing commission that wanted to buy merchant ships from US builders in 1941, while the United States was still technically a neutral nation in the war. In nautical language, the *Whidden* was a three-island, two-deck ship, with a poop deck, bridge deck, and forecastle and two hatches in each well accessing the four cargo holds. The nameboards hung amidships tell onlookers the ship's name, and the stern view shows she was armed with a medium-caliber gun. The presence of the gun probably provided the 23 crewmen a feeling of protection but would have struck little fear in the hearts of an enemy. (Both, JDH.)

In the summer of 1944, welding work continued at night on the *Hidalgo*. She was launched in July, sponsored by Mildred Pepper, wife of prominent US senator Claude Pepper. The *Hidalgo* was a Maritime Commission–built vessel but was taken over by the Navy as AK-189, an Alamosa-class cargo ship. *Hidalgo* was taken to the Gulf of Mexico for finishing, but her naval commissioning did not come until August 4, 1945. She transited the Panama Canal, but by then the war had ended, and the ship was ordered to Norfolk Naval Base and subsequently decommissioned. In April 1946, *Hidalgo* was sold to a Turkish company and became the merchantman *Rize*. (SPL.)

Contemporary photographs of shipyard activity give viewers a good ideal of the size and complexity of the C1s. They were 338 feet long and had a 50-foot beam and a 7,400-ton displacement. At 11 knots, the ships had a range of over 14,000 miles. The crew was normally 35. The Duluth-Superior–built versions of these ships were C1-M-AV1, a variation of the standard C1 design to allow for a shallower draft. This combination of long range and shallower draft was planned for interisland work in the Pacific, a war yet to be won in early 1945. Under construction in these images is the USS *Gwinnett*, which served in the Navy as AK-185. Workers are on the ladder and upper deck in the photograph at right, as are the welders on the right. Notable in the photograph below are the size of the transverse bulkhead, the size of the stern section, and the stern of another C1 behind. (Both, SPL.)

37

The Walter Butler Duluth yard is ready to launch the *Marlin Hitch* in August 1945. The photograph is an unusual one of a launching, as it shows not the ship but the crowd assembled to watch. A launching, of course, signified the completion of a significant amount of work and was a cause of celebration. The large crowd is obvious in the photograph, and the raised platform and piano on the right side may be noted. Also of note is the work gang taking a break on the partly completed bow section of the C1 on the next slip. The *Marlin Hitch* was completed too late to play a role in World War II. (BVC.)

The *Hawser Eye* shows the classic lines of the C1 ships in this and the following two photographs, some fine views of the launching of one of these 5,000-deadweight-ton vessels. The C1, like many World War II ship designs, had a number of variations. A total of 239 were delivered from 10 different shipyards. The C1-M-AV1 was the type built in Duluth-Superior. In this view, workers are on the right doing final preparation, on the left are the clean and open launching way, and the Maritime Commission's Award of Merit is displayed on the bow. (BVC.)

The *Hawser Eye*, as viewed from her port side above, is just minutes away from christening and launching. Notable here is the platform at the bow with flags of the Allied nations flying, and a few of the launch party have arrived. They await the rest of the group, and the sign welcomes the ship's sponsor, Veronica O'Konski, wife of Alvin O'Konski, the congressman representing northern Wisconsin. The workers who will do the labor of getting the ship down the ways are ready and waiting. After speeches and smashing the traditional champagne bottle against the hull to send the ship into the water, she is afloat in the picture below. A tug has already hooked on to tow the *Hawser Eye* to another dock for final work. One of the bridges connecting Duluth with Superior can be seen in the background. (Both, BVC.)

In June 1945, the *Dragonfly* was ready to be launched. The platform for the dignitaries is being readied, and many last-minute details always needed attention before the ceremonies and the launch. Two large cranes on flatcars have been brought alongside, and notable too is the long gangway giving workers access from the dock to the weather deck. The symbol just beneath the ship's name is the Butler coat of arms. (BVC.)

The C1 *Midland* is pictured shortly after launch in the early spring of 1945. This ship is a good example of the difficulty sometimes encountered in tracing the history of a particular ship. She was known as the *Coastal Harbinger*, *Midland*, *AK-195*, and *Union Banker* during her lifetime at sea. She did not see World War II service and was scrapped in 1970. (BVC.)

Of the many C1 freighters built, some were loaned to allied governments, some were operated by the US War Shipping Administration, and a large number were taken by the US Navy for cargo hauling, designated by an AK hull number. This splendid photograph of the USS *Gadsden* (AK-182) shows a C1 in war paint, the Navy's standard haze gray. Launched in April 1944, she went into service in the Pacific in early 1945, taking ammunition and frozen meat to the fleet base at Ulithi Atoll. She spent the remainder of the year as an ammunition ship servicing the fleet, and at war's end, she was laid up at Naval Base Norfolk and subsequently sold to a Korean shipping firm. (SPL.)

Walter Butler's Duluth shipyard was located west of the downtown area in the neighborhood known as Riverside. Ships launched there went into the St. Louis River, which gave clear and direct access to Lake Superior via the St. Louis and Superior Bays. From December through mid-April, ice was a factor in launches and trial runs for new ships. The *Frank Dale* is seen here with her hull complete but her upper works still to be finished. Ice on the ground, the workers' heavy clothing, and the wind-whipped flags all speak to the cold weather that Lake Superior shipyards had to face. (JDH.)

In this undated photograph, an N3 cargo ship steams through the Duluth Ship Canal into a choppy Lake Superior. The vessel is not identified but is certainly out of the Butler Shipyard. The life rafts and gun on the stern are noticeable, as is the open hatch over the rear hold. She also shows the gray paint to give the ship low visibility in the haze of the sea. This is how the ships looked on their way to war. (BVC.)

Three

SHIPYARDS AND WORKERS

The men and women who worked in the Duluth-Superior shipyards were all recruited from northern Wisconsin and Minnesota. Most had little or no experience with welding, plumbing, carpentry, or electrical work, and virtually none had any background in shipbuilding. They were, however, quick learners, and the shipyards became extremely efficient. A photograph from the summer of 1943 shows a crew at Walter Butler's Superior yard posing before a billboard touting the completion of 18 ships. This undoubtedly refers to the number of N3-S-A1 cargo vessels built at that yard. The Walter Butler Company of St. Paul built a new shipyard while also absorbing the existing Lake Superior Shipbuilding Company. The caricatures of Hitler, Hirohito, and Mussolini on the lower part of the board are hard to see but humorous nonetheless. (BVC.)

Superior's Globe Shipyard was a new facility incorporated in the autumn of 1941 by a group of businessmen in that city. Built from scratch on a piece of unused bayfront property, Globe expanded rapidly, and a photographer once said he almost needed a motion picture camera to keep up. Globe would go on to build 29 ships of three different types before war's end. The photograph above, from March 1942, shows the yard very much uncompleted but with the keels of three ships already laid down along the water's edge. Taken one year later, the photograph below exhibits a yard in full operation, and the construction of Globe's first patrol frigate, USS *Covington*, had just begun, as can be clearly seen. The coal yard in back is gone, but the bridge crane is still there as of this writing. (Both, JDH.)

Globe took over this unused building on Superior's waterfront for indoor work, storage, and necessary office space. Notable here are the Globe Shipbuilding Company sign atop the structure and, in the lower left, the modest sign marking the office entrance. (JDH.)

Marine Iron and its neighbor, Zenith Shipyard, were established facilities that became immersed in wartime construction. They were located on Superior Bay near downtown Duluth and built similar types of ships. Marine Iron, seen in this prewar photograph, had built several small harbor craft for the Army Corps of Engineers before the wartime contracts brought expansion. (KML.)

Zenith Dredge was established in 1905 to do harbor dredging and dock work but entered the shipbuilding business in 1941. The photograph above shows the yard itself being expanded before shipbuilding could begin, probably in the spring of 1941. The hills still look rather bare in this early season, and the hilltop tower at right center is the Enger Tower, a Duluth landmark dedicated in 1939 by Crown Prince Olav of Norway. The photograph below was taken several months later and shows the Zenith yard with buildings still under construction. The welding shed is at the left and the boxcars in the back evidence the importance of rail access to bring heavy steel to the shipyards. (Both, DPL.)

The Barnes-Duluth Shipbuilding Company was a major refurbishment of an existing World War I–era yard on Duluth's west end. A prominent Duluth businessman, Julius Barnes, acquired a $4 million–plus contract to build tanker ships and took out loans to rehabilitate the old shipyard. A dozen T1 tankers were built, then eight N3 cargo ships, and then seven smaller tankers. Because of a heavy debt load, Barnes-Duluth struggled financially and, in late 1943, was taken over by Walter Butler, who then operated it as Walter Butler Duluth. The photograph above shows construction of Barnes-Duluth just beginning in 1941, with the slips into which ships will be launched prominent and an existing building to the right. The picture at right is dated December 17, 1941, and shows a crane hoisting roof elements to the new shed. The Great Northern Railroad logo is prominent on the boxcar. (Both, KML.)

Shipbuilding went on 24 hours a day and, although the time and amount work varied, there was always pressure to meet contract deadlines and a shipyard was never quiet. During World War II, welding quickly replaced riveting as the method of construction, as it was faster, saved weight, could be learned more quickly, and needed less labor. The female worker image of Rosie the Riveter that entered the popular imagination might have been Wendy the Welder. This undated photograph from the Walter Butler Superior yard gives a spectacular view of night works in a World War II shipyard. (SPL.)

The photograph may be undated but the season is obvious as Butler Superior workers lay off shipbuilding to do other necessary work. Dealing with snow and ice for part of the year was certainly a handicap for all the Great Lakes shipbuilders. (SPL.)

The caps and coats on these workers clearly reflect weather conditions. The back of the photograph reads, "Men of Walter Butler Shipbuilders homeward bound from their work in the yard at Superior. It was cold working but the weather doesn't stop our men." (SPL.)

Several new techniques for building ships were developed in World War II, and modular construction and welding were perhaps the most significant. With modular construction, large sections of a ship were built separately and then assembled. A large section of the upper decks and bow is being hoisted into the hull here, and once positioned, it will be welded into place. Precisely aligning a many-ton section to within a fraction of an inch was a skilled task. (SPL.)

Not everything always went according to plan. Here, the crane has failed during construction of a C1 vessel and, despite the seeming cold of winter, a number of workers cannot resist the role of onlooker. (SPL.)

An undated and unidentified photograph can still convey a message and, in this case, the message seems to be "oh well, some days are like that." The pickup truck with "WBS" on the door is a tip-off that the location is Walter Butler Superior, but the owner of the unfortunate automobile remains a mystery. (SPL.)

By early 1942, Marine Iron was well under way with Coast Guard cutter construction, and yard infrastructure was proceeding as well. Here, pipefitters are using the relatively new arc welding technique. (DPL.)

The *John Arey*, an N3 coal burner, was built for Britain and launched in 1942. Launchings were, of course, occasions of high ceremony, and here one of the Butler Superior workers stands ready with a ceremonial axe to cut the last line holding the ship and so send it down the ways. It was all symbolism of course. The axe he is holding would scarcely scratch the cable holding the ship in place. (SPL.)

Millions of men in the armed forces meant a labor shortage in defense industries during the war, and millions of women stepped in to fill that gap. Women now worked in thousands of jobs that heretofore were thought to be for men only. This all-female Globe Ship Builders crew is probably a team from a particular area of the shipyard but is otherwise unidentified. Federal law stated the women were to be paid the same as men for equal work, but nationwide it was often not the case. (JDH.)

Shipyards could be dangerous places to work. Heavy things kept getting moved around, and there was noise, weather, slippery footing, ladders, and heights. Hot things and sharp things and hoses and cables to trip over were everywhere. Workers were constantly reminded of the need for safety, but accidents did happen. All shipyards, therefore, had a dispensary or first aid station of some sort where medical attention could be given. The photograph above shows the snowed-in Butler Superior emergency hospital, and below is a staged publicity shot of doctor, nurse, and patient. The patient does not appear to be in serious pain or danger in this case. (Both, SPL.)

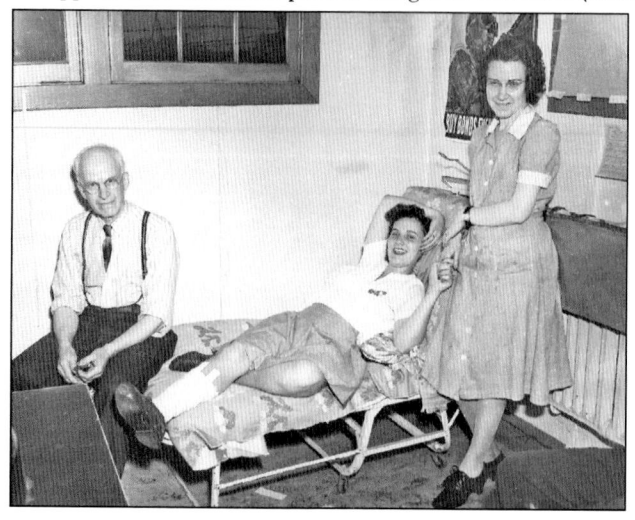

The Butler and Globe yards were big enough to have their own bands composed of volunteers from the ranks of their workers. They usually provided patriotic music at ship launchings, and the Butler band at right is on parade, led by a color guard. The Butler marching band was even provided with its own distinctive uniforms. (BVC.)

This band, assembled for a Butler Superior ship launching, is considerably less formal than the marching band. The saxophonist on the right is clearly a yard worker, while the attire of the trumpet player on the left implies upper management. The bands provided entertainment at employee parties and ship launchings and were generally good for morale. (BVC.)

The Globe band is assembled here to add music for the launching of the USS *Nicollet* on July 31, 1944. The director's attire implies a company official or office worker, and the clothing and hard hats speak to workers laying down their tools for a while to become band members for the event. The young girl in the center is a mystery, and there are plenty observers in the back. The *Nicollet*, as the Navy's AK-199, went on to serve in the Pacific. (JDH.)

This photograph is of a Walter Butler Shipyard luncheon, one of many held to celebrate the launching of one of its vessels. The location is probably the Kitichi Gami Club in Duluth but is otherwise unidentified. Entertainment was normally provided for honored guests and members of the launching party, and a piano and accordion are seen here. The accordion player is in the uniform of the Butler Shipyard Band, and his shoulder patch is a stylized V representing a ship hull and the lettering on the patch reads, "We Build Ships, the Walter Butler Shipbuilder's Band." (BVC.)

Butler shipyard's dancing girls were quite a spectacle. They were part of an entertainment evening staged by Butler employees. The *Superior Evening Telegram* reported that the play *Abby's Irish Rose*, the Butler male chorus, and the Butler 35-piece band would have the "added attractiveness" of the dancing girls on the programs. (SPL.)

To keep up worker morale and foster a sense of community, the larger shipyards sponsored a variety of hobby clubs and sports teams. There were men's and women's bowling teams, softball teams, and, of course, music. The Butler basketball team, in an undated photograph, poses for a team picture to display the trophy it has won. (BVC.)

Employee social activities included ever-popular picnics and, as at many American picnics, an impromptu softball game developed. A beer bottle seems to be evident (it was Wisconsin, after all), and of note is the garbage can lid used has home plate. Most notable in this photograph, however, is the batter, the somewhat formally dressed president of the company, Robert Butler. Butler was politically well connected and after the war served for a time as the US ambassador to Australia. (BVC.)

ZENITH BULLETIN

FEBRUARY 19, 1943

WOMEN WORKERS WANTED!

TO ALL EMPLOYEES:

Inasmuch as the War Manpower Commission, together with the Selective Service Board, will have more and more regulations and restrictions affecting the male personnel in our shipyard, it is necessary for us to take steps immediately to introduce women workers in so far as humanly possible in the various activities of the shipyard.

Therefore, the Management will start, on or about April 1st, weather permitting, to set aside certain sections of the shipyard to be used exclusively for women workers.

The program now contemplated includes women hand and machine burners, tackers and welders, layers-out, and assemblers.

The various Vocational Schools throughout Minnesota and Wisconsin, as well as private occupational schools, governmental employment agencies, etc., will be contacted to the end that women can be put in training for shipyard work at the earliest possible moment.

The Zenith Dredge Company wants to give the first opportunity to the women members of the families of its present employees. Therefore, if any of you have sisters, wives, or other relatives who could perform this work without interfering with their home and family lives - we urge that you have them contact Dan Wright or Bill Haburt and obtain full particulars as to how they can qualify for this work.

We realize that if the female members of the families of our present workers can fill these jobs it will add greatly to our war effort and be a means of conserving gasoline, tires, etc.

The Management feels certain that the whole-hearted cooperation of the shipyard workers will follow once they understand that this move is made solely in the interest of our country's war effort to obtain the maximum production results from all citizens of our country -- both male and female.

                - STEPHEN G. ROCKWELL -
                  General Manager

IT WONT BE LONG NOW!!!

OLD MOTHER HUBBARD WENT TO THE CUPBOARD TO BORROW HER DAUGHTER'S BEST DRESS—BUT WHEN SHE GOT THERE, ONLY SOME TROUSERS WERE THERE DAUGHTER'S A WELDER AT ZENITH, I GUESS!

Nearly all the shipyards published an in-house newspaper. The quality and formats differed greatly but they had in common news for the workers pertaining to events, shipyard policies and rules, results of sports contests, and exhortations to work safely, not miss days of work, and buy war bonds. Butler published *News and Views,* Globe had *Around the Globe,* and Zenith had *Zenith Bulletin,* seen here. The front-page article states a need for women workers, and the cartoon shows the latest fashion as bib overalls. The Glass Block was a well-known Duluth department store. (JDH.)

Four

TUGBOATS AND AUXILIARIES

Incorporated in May 1941, the Globe Shipyard was a new venture by Superior businessmen to take advantage of the plentiful Maritime Commission contracts being offered under the Emergency Shipping Program. Globe's first contract was for five large oceangoing tugboats and was quickly followed by a contract for five more. These 10 tugs were designated V4-M-A1, and all were delivered in 1943. This class of tugs was named after American lighthouses. They were government-owned but were operated by the Moran Towing Company of New York, probably the most experienced such company in the country. The MV (motor vessel) *Farallon* was essentially complete in January 1943 and is seen here at the Globe dock. Her layout is identical to all others of this class. (JDH.)

The sequence of photographs on this and the following three pages shows how the structure of these large tugs was built up from keel laying to launching. Here, the heavy-duty keel of the *Farallon* is set and a rear bulkhead has just been hoisted into place. (JDH.)

The *Point Sur*, pictured in May 1942, was Globe's first V4 tug, and she was christened not with champagne but a bottle of Northern Beer, brewed in Superior. The heavily built-up keel had to be strong to absorb the stress that the tug was going to endure. (JDH.)

The *Trinidad Head* has had seven transverse bulkheads set in place plus a few forward ribs. Two years after this photograph, the *Trinidad Head* would play a significant role in the D-day landings of June 6, 1944, when she towed huge concrete sections of an artificial harbor across the English Channel. (JDH.)

The *Trinidad Head* is seen here not quite a month after the previous picture was taken. Most of the hull ribs are in place, and the interior bulkheads are in place as well. The V4 tugs were 195 feet long, had a beam of about 37 feet, and drew not quite 16 feet of water when loaded. (JDH.)

In late September 1942, work on the hull of the *Wood Island* was well along, and the workers nearby and in the ship's structure give a good perspective on her size. Launched on Christmas Eve 1942, she proved the war industry knew no holidays. (JDH.)

The *Trinidad Head* is seen here on blocks with her launch imminent. Of note here, too, is the ring around the propeller. This was a Kort nozzle, a shaped ring that increased the speed of water flow through it and thus gave extra power for no additional use of fuel. At speeds above about 10 knots, this device loses its effectiveness, but a tugboat's business is power at low speed. (JDH.)

The *Sands Point* has just hit the water in April 1943, keenly observed by a group of yard workers. The V4s were powered by a 2,300-horsepower diesel that turned a single propeller. Their top speed was 14 knots, but when towing, which was much of the time, they made about six knots. They could carry 538 tons of oil, which gave them an impressive range of 19,000 miles. (JDH.)

The *Trinidad Head* splashed on September 19, 1942. After her service in the Normandy landings, she continued to be a hardworking tug, towing a torpedoed destroyer back to England, then several ammunition barges back to northern France, and then towing a disabled 19,000-ton tanker almost 3,500 miles, a job that took a little over 19 days. (JDH.)

This photograph shows the *Point Cabrillo*, launched in September, on Christmas Eve 1942. Her deckhouse and machinery are works in progress, but because of winter ice, she would not sail to the ocean until fair weather in 1943. *Point Cabrillo* and her sister V4 tugs all made the journey across the whole of the Great Lakes and the St. Lawrence River system into the Atlantic—a distance of over 2,300 miles. (JDH.)

This August 23, 1943, photograph shows the sizable difference of design between a tug and a patrol frigate. One was built for power and endurance, the other for speed. The contract to build the 10 V4 tugs was being completed, but Globe now had a contract to build eight patrol frigates, and the USS *Covington* was the first one completed. The tug is not identified but the photograph is a splendid look at the differences between two ships with very different tasks. (JDH.)

| Number thirteen | The Globe Shipbuilding Company, Superior, Wis. | June, 1943 |

Her Colors Flying, Globe's No. 1 Joins V Fleet

PRETTY AS A PICTURE, and ready to take her place in the United Nations' fight for victory. That aptly describes the M. V. Point Sur, already delivered to the U. S. Maritime Commission, and as her powerful motors drive her to far distant points on the globe, Globeship pushes her sisterships to the point where they, too, will take their place in the Victory Fleet.

Covington Delegation Arrives Early-Launching Long Way Off

The girl who was all dressed up and had no place to go didn't have anything on a trio of Covington, Ky., residents who traveled nearly 900 miles to launch a ship at the Globe—only to find that the vessel won't be ready to hit the water for several weeks.

Covington's city manager, Jack Maynard, his wife, and Miss Mckie Phillips, outstanding honor student of her high school at Covington, comprised the delegation from the Blue Grass state, and through a mix-up in signals between the Navy and the U. S. Maritime Commission they arrived approximately seven weeks ahead of the launching date.

Originally the Corvette Covington was to have been launched June 15, or at least that was what City Manager Maynard's invitation to participate in the launching ceremonies declared.

Disappointed over their long journey for naught, Covington's representatives took the misunderstanding good-naturedly, and Mrs. Maynard's chief complaint was "I wish I'd brought my fur coat with me."

Globe officials were sorry the Covington wasn't ready to plunge down the ways, but next time will make certain that all interested parties are correctly informed as to the launching date.

As a special favor to the Covington delegation, "Around the Globe" will personally talk to the weatherman in hopes of getting a warm day for the launching, and maybe Mrs. Maynard won't have to bring along the fur coat she was wishing she had on this trip.

The shipyard newspaper, *Around the Globe*, proudly announced that the yard's first V4 tug was on its way to war service. The tugs did their wartime duty well, and their crews had high praise for their sturdiness, but many did not last long after peace came in 1945. There was not a civilian market for hundreds of surplus tugboats large and small. While none of the V4s survive today, the Superior Public Museum's display aboard the museum ship SS *Meteor* does house some artifacts. Before the *Scotch Cap* was scrapped in 1983, her wheel, Chadburn, nameboard, and a few other items were saved are on display. (SPL.)

Although Zenith Dredge is best remembered for the 180-foot Coast Guard cutters that it built, several other necessary but unsung vessels came from the Zenith yard, too. In July 1942, the *Duluth News Tribune* reported that Zenith Dredge had won a contract to build Navy tankers. By September, work was underway, and the first was launched in March 1943. The ship pictured here was the first of them, the *YW-85*. The Navy's YW designation was for coastal or harbor tankers that were designed to transport liquid cargo to shallower harbors where large vessels could not operate. In the advance across the Pacific, American personnel garrisoned many small islands, and they needed fresh water. (JDH.)

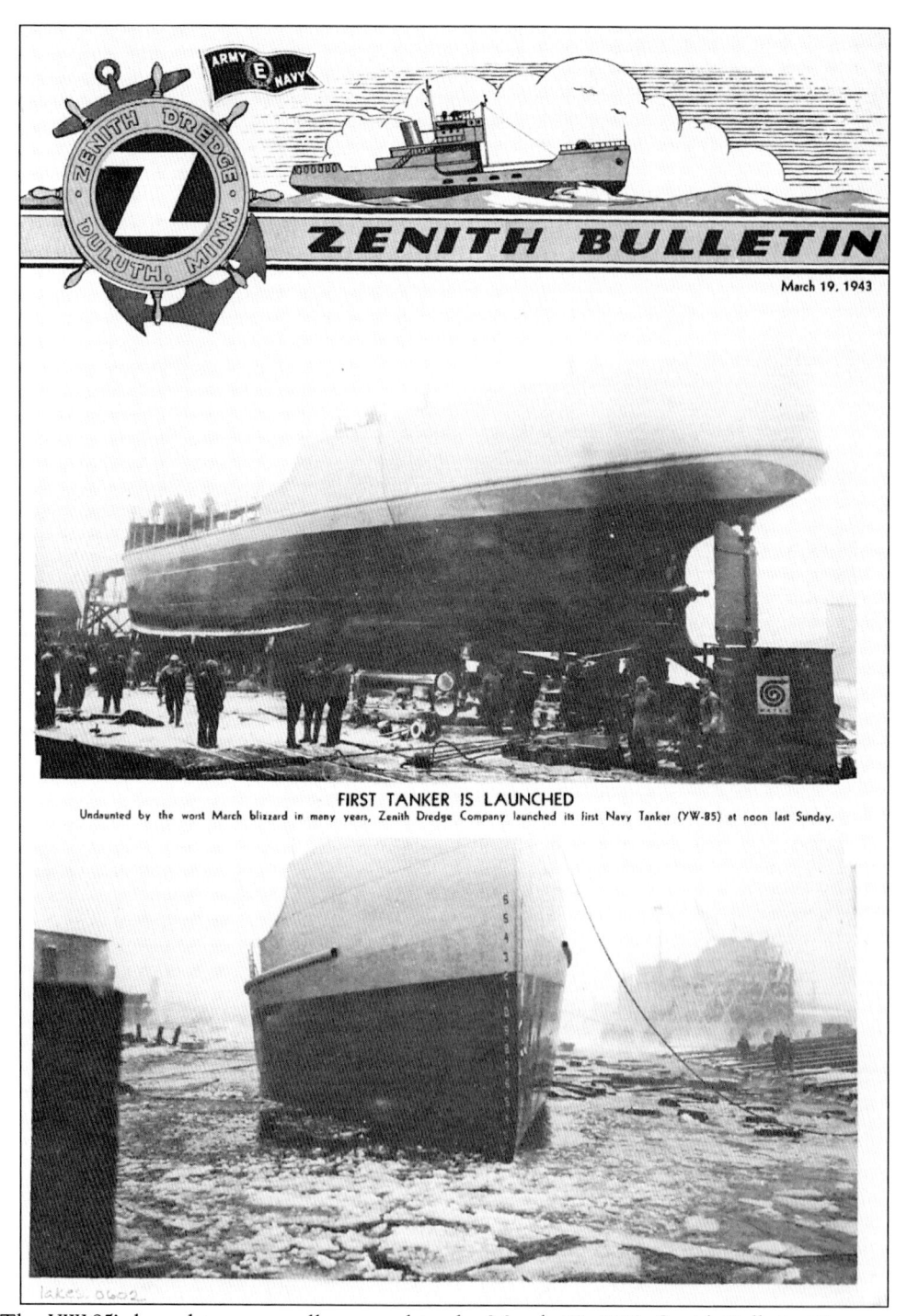

FIRST TANKER IS LAUNCHED
Undaunted by the worst March blizzard in many years, Zenith Dredge Company launched its first Navy Tanker (YW-85) at noon last Sunday.

The *YW-85*'s launching was well reported in the March 19, 1943, *Zenith Bulletin*. Two great pictures show the hazy conditions and floating ice, and the picture line indicates the worst March blizzard in years has just blown through. The YWs were 165 feet long, 32 feet wide, and drew 15 feet. They had a single propeller turned by a diesel of 500 to 600 horsepower, depending on the exact engine. (JDH.)

These drawings show two Zenith vessels, the YW-85 water tanker (above) and the YN-119, a net layer (below). They were done by Felix Ilenda, a Zenith safety department employee. Ilenda was a talented amateur artist who enjoyed sketching the vessels built in his shipyard, and he made these sketches, and others, available for Zenith employees to purchase. The stated price was 65¢ each or three for $1.50. (Both, SPL.)

The YN class ships, four of which were built by Zenith, were net layers, which meant they installed and serviced heavy steel anti-torpedo nets to protect harbor entrances and ships at anchor. The YN-119 was redesigned USS *Tunxis* (AN-90). The photograph clearly shows a derrick-like structure and lifting gear on the bow. The ship's crew was four officers and 42 enlisted men, and they all had to be adept at using block-and-tackle gear and winches. Raising and lowering hundreds of yards of heavy steel mesh netting was arduous work. The ship was powered by a 1,200-horsepower diesel, was 168 feet long, and carried a defensive gun in a tub aft. (JDH.)

Industrial output in World War II demanded work from small companies as well as those that were larger and better known, and this was as true of shipbuilding as anywhere else. A well-established Duluth company, Walker Jamar did many kinds of specialized sheet metal fabrication for the shipyards. Its offices were in Duluth's Canal Park area and, like all northland businesses, it sometimes had deal with heavy snow. Weather was a factor the shipyards had to take into account in building ships and moving them to the oceans. (Both, courtesy of the Jamar family.)

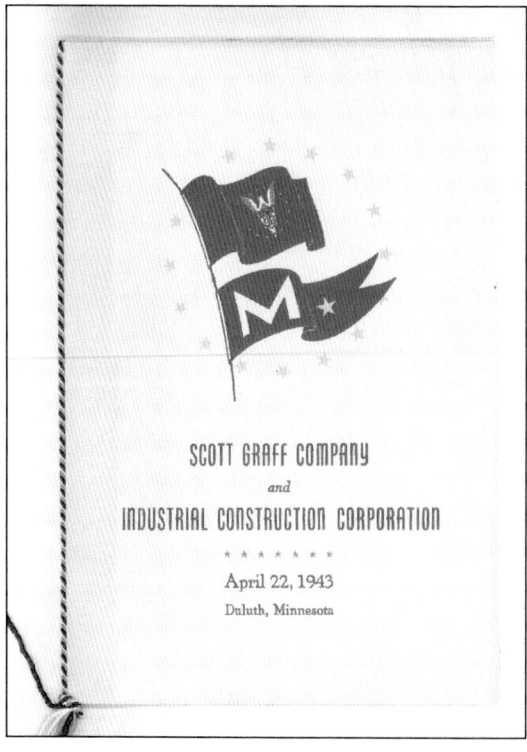

Another small firm that made a large contribution was the Scott-Graff Company. Established as a sawmill in 1870, the company evolved into a maker of various wood products. In the spring of 1942, Scott-Graff obtained a Maritime Commission contract to build fifty 78-foot-long wooden barges for a price of $1,336,494. Seen here is one of the nonmotorized barges under construction. The firm also won a large contract to build prefabricated houses, which were sent by rail to Burlington, Iowa. A large Army ammunition plant there had hired hundreds of new workers, and they need housing. World War II was a complex effort on a national scale. In April 1943, Scott-Graff was honored for its work with the Maritime Commission's M Award, given for overall excellence in meeting contract goals. (Both, KML.)

Five

LAKERS, TANKERS, AND CUTTERS

The *Ashland* was a Great Lakes freighter built with the classic design of those vessels. The ship's bridge and all command functions were housed forward, and crew accommodations were in the aft structure. Steam powered, the engines were below the prominent smokestack aft. With heavy frost on her bow, she is seen here entering port. These vessels, also known as bulk carriers, plied the Great Lakes during the war and were absolutely vital to the American cause. The primary raw material for the steel industry was the iron ore from northern Minnesota, and it was these ships that carried it from Duluth-Superior to the steel mills of Ohio, Pennsylvania, and Illinois. These Great Lakes freighters were not built in Duluth-Superior yards either before or during the war, but they were a constant presence and a fundamental part of Twin Ports shipping. (JDH.)

The *Robert C. Stanley* was a Great Lakes bulk carrier built for the Maritime Commission and operated by a private shipping company. The need to greatly expand steel production and to do so rapidly meant an attendant increase in the ability to transport the raw material. So essential was the flow of iron ore that 16 of these ships were contracted for early in the war and delivered in 1943. These ships, designated L6-S-A1, were built in shipyards at Cleveland and Ashtabula, Ohio, and at River Rouge, Michigan. This photograph shows the *Stanley* at a massive iron ore dock. Railroad tracks carried loaded hopper cars all the way out on the dock, the iron ore was dumped into huge pockets, or bins, inside the V-shaped structure; the chutes, seen in the up position, were lowered to the hatches of the ships; and the ore flowed down into the holds by gravity. (JDH.)

River Rouge, Michigan, was the birthplace of the *Robert C. Stanley*, and this splendid photograph gives a good impression of the size of these bulk carriers. The L6 freighters were 620 feet long, 60 feet wide, and had four massive holds. Access to load and unload these holds was through 18 steel hatches that each measured 38 by 11 feet. Power came from triple expansion steam engines producing 2,500 horsepower. (JDH.)

The *Stanley* suffered several mishaps during her life on the Lakes. On her first voyage across Lake Superior to Duluth, in November 1943, she suffered a severe crack in the hull, and the crew strung cables from bow to stern to relieve the stress until port could be reached and repairs made. After the war, she suffered a fire and a grounding, as well as the 1967 collision illustrated here. A following ship clearly had not stopped in time. (JDH.)

The *Fayette Brown* was one of the older Lakers. Built in 1910, she carried on all through World War II as well as the Korean War. The end came in 1964, when she sank while in tow to a ship-breaker's yard. The *Brown* is shown here, probably at Superior, unloading coal. Coal was in demand for home heating as well as industrial uses during the war, and most coal came from Pennsylvania and West Virginia. It was common to send ships up the Lakes with coal and send them back with iron ore. (KML.)

This unidentified photograph shows clearly the scale of the Lakers, the size of the hatches, and the clamshells and cranes for the unloading process, whether the cargo be coal or iron ore. (KML.)

The *J. Burton Ayers* was one of the 16 L6 bulk carriers built for the wartime emergency. The ship is seen here unloading coal, probably in Superior. A ship of this type could carry about 16,000 tons. The bulk cargoes were most commonly coal or iron ore but could also be limestone or grain. Notable here is the proximity of the railcars to the dock and the unloading equipment, as fast turnaround time for these vessels was a must. There was steel to be made and a war to be won. (Both, JDH.)

The *John T. Hutchinson*, a Cleveland-built L6-S-A1 bulk carrier, sails downbound in this wartime photograph. The ship is riding low in the water, and she is almost certainly carrying iron ore that will be unloaded in one of the Ohio ports and then taken by rail to feed the steel mills of Pittsburgh. In this view, the building partially seen on the right was, and still is, Army Corps of Engineers' offices, the lift bridge is very much in use as of this writing, and the location of the warehouse and silo at center is the site of a modern hotel. (JDH.)

The Barnes-Duluth Shipbuilding Company was incorporated in May 1941 and began rehabilitating an old World War I–era shipyard. In November, it received its first contract, a Maritime Commission order for eight small oil tankers. These were Maritime Commission designs designated T1-M-A1. This yard would eventually build 12 of these tankers, all delivered between May and October 1943. The *Cromwell*, seen here, is doing sea trials and pushing up a decent bow wave just off shore in mid-1943. All crew accommodations are aft, and the forward three-fourths of the ship contains gasoline storage tanks and attendant deck piping and plumbing. (JDH.)

The T1 tankers were specific designs to carry gasoline into small harbors, and a total of 113 were built at seven shipyards. The 12 built by Barnes-Duluth were all sent to Britain under the Lend-Lease Act and so never carried a US Navy designation or number. The photograph at left is of the *Cromwell* and shows the large space for gasoline tankage below the weather deck. Completion is still several months away. Below is the *Mannington*, whose construction is much further along. Both photographs were taken on November 26, 1942. The workers aboard give a good perspective of the ships' size, and the necessary piping for a gasoline tanker is taking form on the deck. The *Mannington*'s launch was about five and a half months in the future at the time of this photograph. (Both, JDH.)

| MRS. CATHERINE WALCZYNSKI
MOTHER - ANDREW ALLOISE
WALCZYNSKI. KILLED IN ACTION,
HICKAM FIELD T. H., DEC. 7,
1941 - CHRISTENER OF
"TARENTUM" | | MRS. CATHERINE MCQUADE BERG
SISTER - ROBERT CAMERON
MCQUADE. KILLED IN ACTION,
PEARL HARBOR T. H., DEC. 7,
1941 - CHRISTENER OF
"MANNINGTON" |

THE BARNES-DULUTH SHIPBUILDING COMPANY

CORDIALLY INVITES YOU AND YOUR GUEST TO BE PRESENT
AT THE LAUNCHING OF THE

UNITED STATES MARITIME COMMISSION TANKERS
"TARENTUM" AND "MANNINGTON"

AT FOUR O'CLOCK
(PROGRAM TO START AT 3:30 P. M.)
JUNE THIRD, NINETEEN HUNDRED FORTY-TWO

FOOT OF SPRING STREET, RIVERSIDE (85TH AVENUE WEST)
DULUTH, MINNESOTA

NOTE: TO AVOID TRAFFIC CONGESTION, PARKING ON GRAND AVENUE IS REQUESTED
PLEASE PRESENT THIS CARD FOR ADMISSION

The shipyard sent out these formal invitations to guests of the *Mannington*'s launch along with sister ship *Tarentum*. The Maritime Commission's Ships for Victory logo was usually used on these occasions, but on this invitation, the sponsors are of particular note. One is the mother of a young man killed at the Air Corps' Hickam Field, and the other is the sister of a sailor killed at Pearl Harbor—both on December 7, 1941. (JDH.)

The *Titusville* is on her building blocks and ready to slide into the water in July 1943. The group of six men posing for a picture beneath the bow seems to be a mix of management and labor, judging from their dress. The *Titusville* and the other tankers were powered by a 720-horsepower diesel engine and were 220 feet long with a beam of 37 feet and draft of 13 feet. (KDH.)

The *Cromwell* seems to be working up to full power as she exits the Duluth ship canal and sails into Lake Superior. The T1 tankers like the *Cromwell* had a crew of eight officers and 50 enlisted men. Accommodations were spartan but livable and a 3-inch gun was mounted aft, though rarely used. The ship's job was to take gasoline to where it was needed, and the Cromwell could carry 12,100 barrels. The definition of a barrel varies, but if the oil industry standard of a 42-gallon barrel is used, these small tankers could carry slightly over half a million gallons of gasoline. (JDH.)

Welcome Aboard

UNITED STATES COAST GUARD CUTTER

WOODRUSH

WLB - 407

In May 1941, the US Coast Guard's fleet badly needed modernization and bids were accepted for a new class of multipurpose ships. The contracts for the new vessels were awarded to Marine Iron and Zenith Dredge, two neighboring and cooperating yards on Duluth's waterfront. The *Zenith Bulletin* later described the mission of the new ships as "anti-submarine warfare, rescuing crews of torpedoed vessels and planes and salvaging the ships and planes, breaking a path through Arctic ice for convoys, patrol and escort duty, and the vital duty of establishing aids to navigation of Allied war vessels no matter how remote the location"—multipurpose to say the least! The last of these ships built was the *Woodrush*, depicted on this brochure for visitors on an open ship day. (JDH.)

This cold January 7, 1943, saw three of the new Coast Guard cutters in the water and another under construction slip side. This view of the Zenith shipyard looks to the northeast, and the downtown area of Duluth is on the right. The two ships at the head of the slip are probably the *Sorrell* and the *Madrona*, both launched in the fall of 1942 and finished in the spring of 1943. These were Cactus-class vessels. (JDH.)

This dramatic double photograph of a Zenith launching is dated July 3, 1942, and shows the cutter *Woodbine*. Her future service as an active cutter would span 30 years. During World War II, she served in the Caribbean and then the Pacific. She was part of the fleet that defeated the Japanese near Guam and, later, Okinawa. After the war, she came back to the Great Lakes and was based in Grand Haven, Michigan. Until her decommissioning in 1972, the *Woodbine*'s work included search and rescue, ice breaking, and buoy tending. (JDH.)

The new cutters from the Zenith and Marine Iron yards were of three different subclasses but all were called "the 180s." They were 180 feet long, 37 feet wide, and drew 12 feet. The 180s were classified as buoy tenders, but their hulls were designed with a rounded bow and sufficient strength for them to do light-duty ice breaking. The photograph was taken after World War II but nicely shows WLB-407, the *Woodrush*, doing just that in the port of Duluth-Superior. The grain silos and the massive iron ore docks in the distance speak to the main business of this port. (JDH.)

The 180s, both during and after the war, were the most common Coast Guard vessels on the Great Lakes. The five Great Lakes are at latitudes where winter is not a kind time, and seasonal storms can be wicked. "The Gales of November" is a well-known local phrase and the name of an annual symposium held in Duluth in November. These two photographs starkly make the point that Coast Guard crews had cold, hard work in the wintertime on the lakes. Above, the *Woodrush*, her bow heavily covered in ice, seems to have just tied up, and the photograph below shows a dock line out. The crewman is certainly concentrating on the task at hand and seems to have made progress in chipping ice off the anchor. (Both, JDH.)

The 180s were classified as buoy tenders, and the Great Lakes' many harbors, rivers, and channels were marked with numerous buoys for safe navigation. While the lakes themselves rarely freeze completely over, the harbors and channels do. Many buoys, therefore, must be taken out in the fall and reset in the spring. It was hard and dangerous work, and the buoys needed to be precisely positioned. The 180s had a deck hoist that could lift 25 tons to bring buoys and their anchors aboard, and here a concrete-block anchor is being lifted. (JDH.)

ZENITH BULLETIN

DECEMBER 4, 1942

"TUPELO" LAUNCHED ON NOVEMBER 30TH

Zenith's 7th boat of the year is pictured as it struck the water at 12:20 P.M. November 30th.

It's the TUPELO, the last Coast Guard Cutter under construction at the Zenith yard... and probably the final boat to be launched this year.

If the weather holds, the first Navy tanker may still be set free this year.

A few minutes previous to this launching, Marine Iron gave the BUTTONWOOD its first taste of water.

ADMIRAL'S VISIT HIGHLIGHTS CEREMONIES

Highlighting the launching of the TUPELO was the visit of Vice Admiral R. R. Waesche, of Washington, D. C. Commandant of the U. S. Coast Guard.

Admiral Waesche is shown here with the sponsors of the launching.

(Left to right:)

Lt. Commander D.G. Morrison,
Commander Beckwith Jordan,
Miss Nancy Hay of St. Louis,
Vice Admiral R. R. Waesche,
Miss Florence Rizzuto,
Commander G. A. Tyler,
Lt. Commander A. L. Ford.

The December 4, 1942, *Zenith Bulletin* features the launching of the *Tupelo* five days earlier. Zenith built 17 and Marine Iron 21 of the 180s, by far more than any other builders. Winter did not stop ship construction in the Twin Ports, and a personal visit by the commandant of the Coast Guard was a newsworthy event. (JDH.)

The *Balsam*, shown here in haze gray war paint, was the first 180 built by Zenith Dredge. She was launched in April 1942 and later in the year went into service in the South Pacific. The wartime crew numbered six officers and 74 enlisted men, although the peacetime crew was somewhat smaller. Armament was a 3-inch deck gun, several machine guns, and depth charges. Two diesel engines powered electric motors that turned the propeller. In June 1944, a Navy flying boat experienced an in-flight fire and made a forced landing near remote Howland Island. The aircraft was a total loss, but the crew had radioed for help, and the *Balsam* rescued them all. It was one small example of the 180s at work. (JDH.)

Six
CELEBRITIES AND SHIP LAUNCHINGS

Launching a ship was its symbolic birth and was always done with ceremony and formality. It was considered a high honor, and by nautical tradition, it was always a woman to be selected as a ship's sponsor. There was normally a prominent platform from which speeches would be given, and the customary bottle of champagne would be smashed on the bow to send the vessel on its way. The ship was frequently decorated with patriotic bunting. In this view, the C1 freighter *Fiador Knot* is ready to launch on April 26, 1945. The Maritime Commission banner is draped from the bow, and flags of the Allied nations are flying. Note that the American flag is at half-staff. Pres. Franklin D. Roosevelt had died 12 days earlier. (BVC.)

On November 20, 1944, Ingrid Bergman addresses a crowd of workers at the Butler Duluth shipyard. Many celebrities backed the war by lending their names to the war bond drives. The sale of these bonds was a way of offsetting the enormous cost of the war without drastic tax increases and encouraging citizens to buy bonds was a high priority. The Swedish actress was one of the best-known film stars of the time, and she made a Duluth stop on her war bond tour. She had been nominated for an Oscar for best actress of 1943 (*For Whom the Bell Tolls*), and her 1942 film *Casablanca* remains one of the most famous of all time. A personality of her stature was sure to draw a crowd, and the photograph above shows it. She urged them to buy bonds and said that she was "thrilled by the beautiful boats." The photograph at left shows the company president, Robert Butler, presenting Bergman with a pin or medal that she seems to happily and graciously accept. (Both, SPL.)

Motion picture stars were favorites to sponsor a ship because of the great media attention that automatically came with such an appearance. The newspaper clipping from May 12, 1945, is an example. The *St. Paul Dispatch* announces Anne Baxter's appearance at the Butler shipyard in Duluth, 130 miles distant, indicating she will sponsor the ship "*Lover's Bend.*" It was an unfortunate typographical error, as the ship's name was *Lever's Bend*. It was one of a group of C1s built by Butler that were named after nautical knots. The photograph below is clearly a publicity shot of Anne Baxter exiting the aircraft on which she flew into Duluth. (Both, BVC.)

Anne Baxter was 22 when she came to the Butler yard, and her star status had just begun to rise. She had become well known thanks to her major role in *The Magnificent Ambersons*, a 1942 film directed by Orson Welles. It is regarded by many critics as an American classic, and Baxter plays one of the two major female roles. At left is a standard ship launching publicity shot taken at the Butler yard. A signboard like this was always set up on the platform with the sponsor's name clearly displayed. Large crowds invariably attended a launching, and a film star was sure to attract more, particularly on a nice day in May. The banner hanging from the bandstand at center reads "We Adore You Anne Baxter—The Butler Shipyard Employees." (Left, SPL; below, BVC.)

In May 1945, Baxter's arrival at the Duluth airport was captured in this publicity photograph. She poses with considerable luggage, including the requisite round hatbox. Her postwar career would include winning an Oscar for best supporting actress of 1946 (*The Razor's Edge*) and being nominated for the best actress Oscar of 1950 (*All about Eve*). The airline logo on the door behind is, of course, Northwest Airlines. A Minnesota–based airline, Northwest began carrying mail and passengers in 1926, and during World War II, it flew routes in the Midwest and Pacific Northwest and pioneered air routes to Alaska. In a 2008 merger, Northwest was absorbed by Delta Air Lines. (BVC.)

Although he was not in Superior to sponsor a ship, Wendell Wilkie visited the Butler shipyard during the winter in late 1943 or early 1944. Wilkie, here meeting shipyard workers, was a political celebrity. He had served with the US Army in France during World War I and later earned a law degree and specialized in public utility matters. In 1933, he was president of Commonwealth & Southern, one of the largest electric utilities in the nation. He opposed many of President Roosevelt's New Deal programs and thus became a significant spokesman for the Republican Party. Wilkie won the Republican nomination for president in 1940 and ran against Roosevelt, who was running for an unprecedented third term. The president won handily, carrying 38 states to his 10, but Wilkie had become well known and, after the United States entered the war, used his prominence to support the war effort. (BVC.)

During his visit to the Butler Superior shipyard, Wendell Wilkie inspected ongoing work, met with management, and lent his name to the need for more production. In the 1940 campaign opposing Roosevelt, Wilkie agreed with the president on the need to send aid to Great Britain and avoided further dividing the nation on that issue, which helped guarantee Britain's survival. Wilkie is shown here walking past the USS *Emporia* (PF-28) locked in the winter ice. She had been launched late in the previous summer and would be sent on her way in 1943. (BVC.)

The band customarily paraded for major launchings, and here, on October 27, 1944, members are formed up for the launch of C1 vessel *Joe P. Martinez*, built at the Butler Duluth facility. Homes in that city's west end can be seen in the background, and the bass drum makes it impossible to mistake this group for any other band, reading "Walter Butler Shipbuilders Superior" and featuring a stylized picture of an N3 ship in the center. (BVC.)

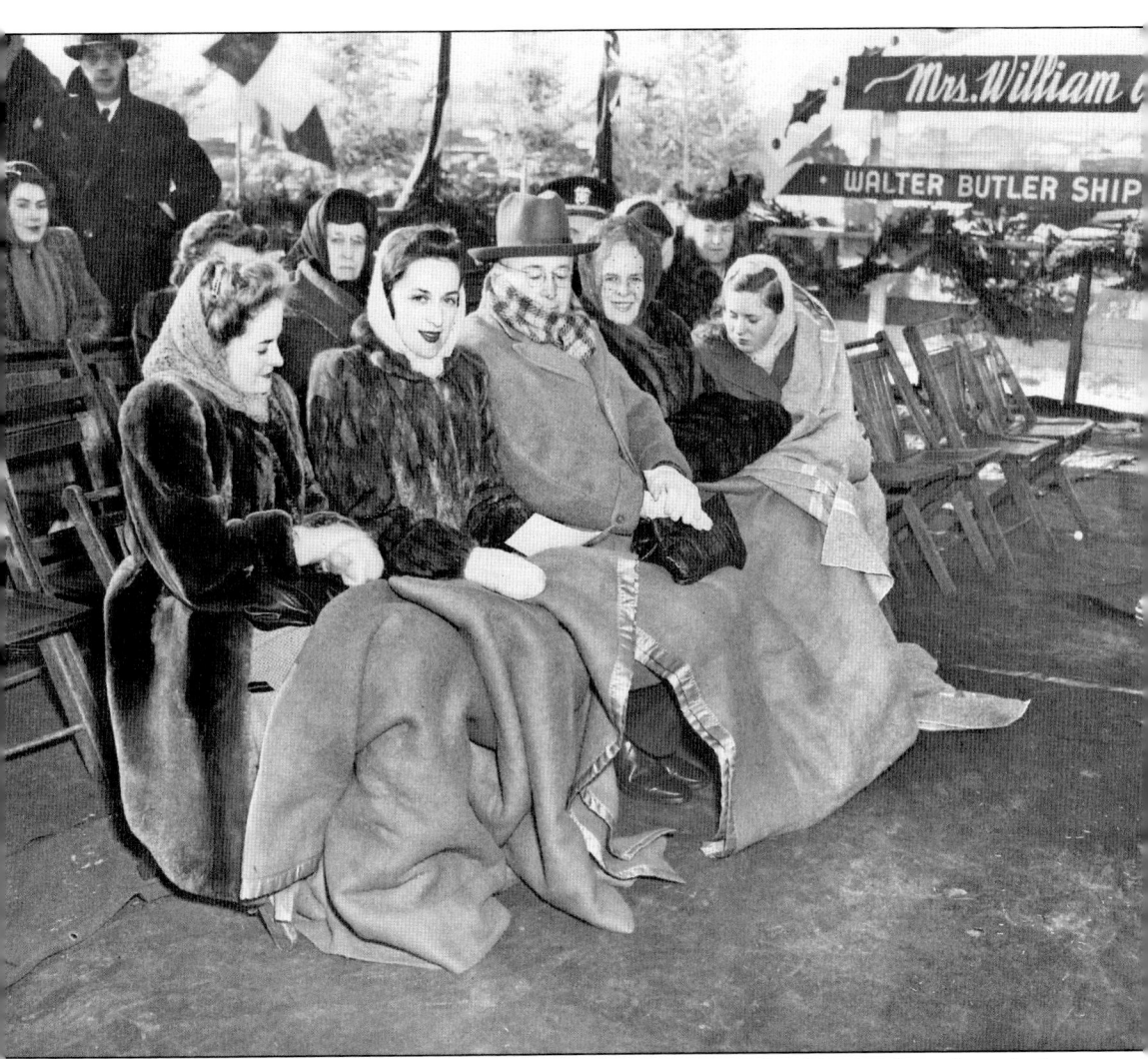

Cold weather did not stop shipyard work or launchings. The USS *Midland* (AK-195) was launched on December 23, 1945. It was a cold day, and the ship was launched into an icy slip. The dignitaries are well bundled up under the blankets, and the signboard honors Mrs. William G. Mitsch, the ship's sponsor, seated second from the left. The AK-195 did not enter service until the very end of the war, so her career was brief. There are no reports of cold-weather launch party casualties. (BVC.)

The wives of prominent politicians, especially those who were members of Congress, were often invited to christen a ship. Alvin O'Konski was the congressman representing the district that covered the whole of northern Wisconsin, including the city of Superior. His wife, Veronica (second from left), is shown here ready to do her duty on launch day, and to the right of her are Dora and Carl Bong, parents of Richard Bong, America's leading combat pilot. The woman at far left is unidentified. (BVC.)

Veronica "Bonnie" O'Konski smashes the traditional bottle of champagne at the moment of launch. She was a Wisconsin native, and her congressman husband, Alvin, served in the House of Representatives from 1943 to 1973. Congressman O'Konski served on the House Armed Forces Committee, which made recognizing him highly desirable for a shipyard dealing with the armed forces. The congressman was also the coauthor of the GI Bill, which aided so many veterans after the war. (BVC.)

Walter Butler Shipbuilders always hosted a formal luncheon for the launch party. Here, Bonnie O'Konski is seated at center with shipyard president Robert Butler to the left of her. The Butler Balladeers often performed, as they do here, with a seemingly happy accordion player doing the accompaniment. (BVC.)

In July 1944, Mildred Pepper made the news as sponsor of the *Hidalgo*, as this contemporary article shows. She was the wife on an influential US senator from Florida, Claude Pepper. The senator stands to the right of his wife below. One of the longest-serving members of Congress ever, Pepper served in the senate and then the House of Representatives between 1934 and his retirement in 1989. He was known as a champion of civil rights and prolabor legislation. (Both, BVC.)

107

Ship sponsors were drawn from the world of business as well as entertainment and government. Helen Hunter, wife of Croil Hunter, the president of Northwest Airlines, sponsored the C1 ship *Shamrock Knot* in March 1944. Croil Hunter headed the airline from 1933 to 1952 and led its expansion from a small regional to a national airline with routes linking Chicago, Minneapolis, and Seattle and serving many smaller cities in the area, such as Duluth. (BVC.)

The banquet luncheon after a launch ceremony was a much-anticipated gala, and Butler Shipbuilders did it well. These two photographs show such an event at the Kitchi Gammi Club, Duluth's premier private club. The photograph above is of the launch party for the *Shamrock Knot*. Helen Hunter is in the white hat on the left exchanging pleasantries with Robert Butler, while Croil Hunter takes in the Butler Balladeers and Margaret Butler (far right), Robert Butler's wife, looks on with enjoyment. The photograph below is undated, but Robert Butler is seated fourth from the right and seems to be the center of attention. (Both, BVC.)

This undated photograph further illustrates the extravagant formality of the events surrounding a ship launch. It did, after all, mark the culmination of considerable work in creating a new ship from paper plans and steel plates. The photograph was taken at the Kitchi Gammi Club's upper hall and of note are the number of guests, the formality of the table settings, and the number of servers. Robert Butler is at the head table in the center. (BVC.)

Launch programs followed a standard format dictated by nautical tradition, but that is not to say that variation was not to be seen. In June 1945, Robert Butler's daughter, Catherine, was given the honor. Maritime tradition dictated only that a sponsor be female; there was no age requirement. The ceremony was themed in honor of the young children of the community, and these two photographs illustrate favorite characters from traditional children's stories and popular cartoon characters. Below, sponsor Catherine hold the traditional bouquet and poses with the kids invited to front-row seats at a Superior yard launch. (Both, BVC.)

Butler Shipyard's work was done under government contract and, therefore, accountability was maintained by on-time delivery of ships and by periodic inspection visits from naval and Maritime Commission officials. This undated photograph from the Butler Superior yard shows, from left to right, Julius Fink, the shipyard's chief inspector for quality control; Robert Butler; Lieutenant Johnson, Naval Bureau of Navigation; Tom Faricy, US Bureau of Shipping; Lieutenant Commander Stone, Naval Bureau of Navigation; and George Dolan, the Butler Shipbuilding public relations man. (BVC.)

The Butler in-house newsmagazine, *News and Views*, published this photograph in the May 1943 issue. It shows the top officials of the shipyard and the visiting heads of the US Maritime Commission, which oversaw all shipbuilding nationwide except that done directly by the Navy. Coming down the ladder, from bottom to top, are Rear Adm. Howard Vickery, vice chairman of the Maritime Commission; Adm. Emory Land, chairman of the Maritime Commission; Robert Butler; Gus Meyer, general superintendent of the shipyard; Lt. William Weber, Admiral Vickery's assistant; and W.E. Spofford, Great Lakes area director, Maritime Commission. (BVC.)

LAUNCHING PARTY

Shown below are the members of the launching party for Zenith's first tanker, YW-85, which was launched last Sunday.

Left to right: A. S. McDonald, chairman of the Board of Zenith Dredge Company; Donald C. MacDonald, president; Commander G. A. Bergman, U.S.N.R.; Mrs. A. S. McDonald, the sponsor of YW-85; E. D. Twiehaus, Bos'n, USN; and Stephen G. Rockwell, general manager of Zenith Dredge.

Start Digging, Chum

The weather has temporarily postponed the Red Cross drive in our yard - but is expected to get underway either late this week or the first part of next week.

REMEMBER - every worker is expected to donate at least 4 hour's pay for this worthy cause.

If you wish these deductions may be made from your paycheck. To make it easier for you men these deductions are being held up until May, when your paychecks will be larger.

← Here's the Only man who can afford to lose his head!

AVOID ACCIDENTS

DATING as far back as 2100 B.C., the christening and launching ceremony originated as an offering to the gods of the elements. At first wine was used, but the Greeks and Romans introduced water as a token of purification. Chinese launching rites are elaborate and have not been changed for centuries. In 18th Century France there was small difference between church baptismal ceremonies and those of sending a ship down the ways on her maiden voyage. Today this religious significance has faded. Only the name is bestowed as the lady sponsor cracks a champagne bottle over the prow. Tradition has it that the *Constitution* balked on the first two attempts to launch her using a water-filled container. But "Old Ironsides" responded nobly when choice old Madeira doused her stout timbers.

Society Brand Clothes
$50.00

Columbia
Clothing Co.
203 WEST SUPERIOR STREET

Come to
ENGER & OLSON INC
19th AVENUE WEST AND SUPERIOR STREET

FOR MODERN IDEAS
IN FURNITURE !

CANAL PARK VISITOR CENTER
COLLECTION Duluth, MN

The Zenith Shipyard was much smaller than Butler, and its launching parties were not quite so elaborate. This page from the March 19, 1943, *Zenith Bulletin* carries a picture of the launch party for the *YW-85* water tanker. A.S. McDonald is listed as chairman of the board, Donald C. McDonald as president; and Mrs. A.S. McDonald as the sponsor of the ship. (JDH.)

This montage was prepared by Walter Butler Superior for an event that gained national, indeed international, attention in May 1943. It could just as well be titled "Five Girls, Five Ships, and One Famous Day." Robert Butler had a finely tuned sense of publicity and in the spring of 1943 came up with a master stroke. In 1934, quintuplets, all girls, had been born to a French Canadian family, the Dionnes, and such was the rarity of the event that the Dionne quintuplets became world-famous. The shipyard had five N3s nearing completion, and with a little planning, they could be launched on the same day. (SPL.)

The Dionne quintuplets came to Superior on a special train and were accompanied by their mother, father, and four siblings. The photograph above shows them being greeted by Robert Butler, and the one below shows them, with an Army escort, being greeted by a group of shipyard workers. Their train journey from Québec to Superior was tracked and reported all the way, and there was great speculation as to whether they would sing "God Bless America" or "The Star-Spangled Banner" and whether they would sing in English or French. Their 16-year-old brother even made the newspapers because he had to stay home and take care of "two beautiful Belgian horses" because he could not leave them alone "just to be an honored guest at a government celebration." (Both, BVC.)

116

On the day of the big event, May 9, 1943, the five girls were seated together, with Robert Butler and other notable guests standing behind. The ships to be launched were earmarked to be sent directly to Great Britain. Five American-built ships being launched by five Canadian girls and all five ships going to England spoke to the international character of the Allies and was a public relations dream. (BVC.)

The event was broadcast live on network radio and shown in theater newsreels, and an estimated 20,000 people crowded into and near the shipyard to see it all. Elzire Dionne said it was the best Mother's Day she had ever had, Oliva Dionne declared himself a proud papa, and Adm. Emory Land, boss of the Maritime Commission, said that with events like these "Hitler doesn't have a snowball's chance." The Dionne family then boarded their special train car to return home. (BVC.)

Of all celebrities that visited Duluth Superior shipyards, probably none was greater that Richard I. Bong, nicknamed "America's Ace of Aces." Dick grew up in Poplar, a small town east of Superior, graduated from Superior High School, and attended college there as well. Having taken private flying lessons, he enlisted in the Air Corps in May 1941 and by 1942 was a first-line fighter pilot flying the twin-engine P-38 Lockheed Lightning, a long-range fighter, out of bases in New Guinea and, later, the Philippines. In November 1943, he was given leave to come home, already famous for shooting down 21 Japanese aircraft in aerial combat. A local hero, Bong was much in demand and made a number of appearances at the shipyards. One of these was at the Globe Shipyard, where he spoke and was presented with a specially fabricated knife from the machine shop. (BVC.)

During his home leave in late 1943 and early 1944, Dick Bong met Marge Vattendahl, a young teacher with whom he fell in love. On returning to the Southwest Pacific, he named his airplane "Marge" and plastered a big picture of her on the nose. How the relationship turned out is clearly shown in this February 10, 1945, photograph. By the time of the wedding, Bong had shot down 40 Japanese aircraft, more "kills" than any other American pilot in the war. (BVC.)

A rather unique wedding cake is obvious in two photographs taken on February 10, 1945. Dick's parents, Carl and Dora, are on the left, with Marge's folks on the right. The ship crowning the wedding cake is quite a good rendition of the C1-M-A1 cargo ships built by Walter Butler Superior. The photograph below clearly shows that the Butler Shipyard helped with the wedding but got some publicity from it as well, because it was a nationally reported event. Dick had become a true American hero and in October 1944 had been awarded the Medal of Honor, the nation's highest military decoration. The good wishes for happy sailing on the cake were, tragically, to be only measured in months. Dick, now a major, had done his combat duty but, at his request, the Air Corps let him continue flying as a test pilot. He was killed when a new jet-propelled aircraft he was testing crashed on August 6, 1945. They had been married not quite seven months. (Both, BVC.)

During his first home leave in late 1943 and early 1944, Bong spoke at the Butler Shipyard in Superior, as this photograph shows. Notable here is the banner overhead congratulating him on being an Army ace in the Pacific. Bong's Air Corps–issue gloves and woolen-collared leather jacket would have been as welcome in the Lake Superior winter as they were flying at high altitude. (BVC.)

In December 1943, Dick paid a visit to the Globe Shipyard, spoke to the employees, and was asked by Pat Connor, a welder in the yard, to autograph this portrait. The Globe's newspaper reported that "the girls had obtained a handsome portrait of the captain prior to his visit and he graciously autographed it for them." There was a bit of good-natured kidding between the "welderette" and the "No. 1 Pin-Up Boy." (BVC.)

Dick Bong visited the Globe yard on January 7, 1944, as an honored guest at the launching of one of Globe's patrol frigates, the USS *Worcester*. He was given the rare privilege of being aboard and riding with the launch crew as the ship went into the water. Bong is very prominently standing on the bow above the American flag. The *Worcester*'s name was changed to USS *Gladwyne* very soon after it was launched, and the *Worcester* name was given to a new light cruiser then under construction in another shipyard. The *Gladwyne* would serve in the Pacific during the last year of the war. (BVC.)

In January 1944, Bong was home between his second and third combat tours. While he was welcomed and feted everywhere, everyone wanted to see him fly his P-38. Taking off from the city of Superior's airport, he few several low passes over the harbor area and the shipyards. This photograph shows a low pass over the Globe Shipyard on or about January 7, 1944. (BVC.)

This photograph of Capt. Dick Bong making a low banking pass over the clearly marked sheds of the Butler Shipyard in Superior is one of the best and most iconic photographs of the war era in Duluth-Superior. The picture's condition is not good, but its immediacy offsets any lack of resolution. It is a beautiful shot of the P-38 with America's Ace of Aces at the controls. (BVC.)

About the Organizations

The Richard I. Bong Veterans Historical Center in Superior, Wisconsin, is a museum centered on the career of Maj. Dick Bong, America's top-scoring ace fighter pilot of World War II. It collects, preserves, and displays artifacts pertinent to that period but honors all veterans of America's conflicts. The centerpiece of the museum is a restored Lockheed P-38 Lightning of the type Bong flew.

The US Army Corps of Engineers operates the Lake Superior Maritime Visitor Center on the Duluth, Minnesota, waterfront. Artifacts and displays there show the current and historical importance of the port of Duluth-Superior. The Lake Superior Marine Museum Association supports the visitor center in telling this history.

DISCOVER THOUSANDS OF LOCAL HISTORY BOOKS FEATURING MILLIONS OF VINTAGE IMAGES

Arcadia Publishing, the leading local history publisher in the United States, is committed to making history accessible and meaningful through publishing books that celebrate and preserve the heritage of America's people and places.

Find more books like this at
www.arcadiapublishing.com

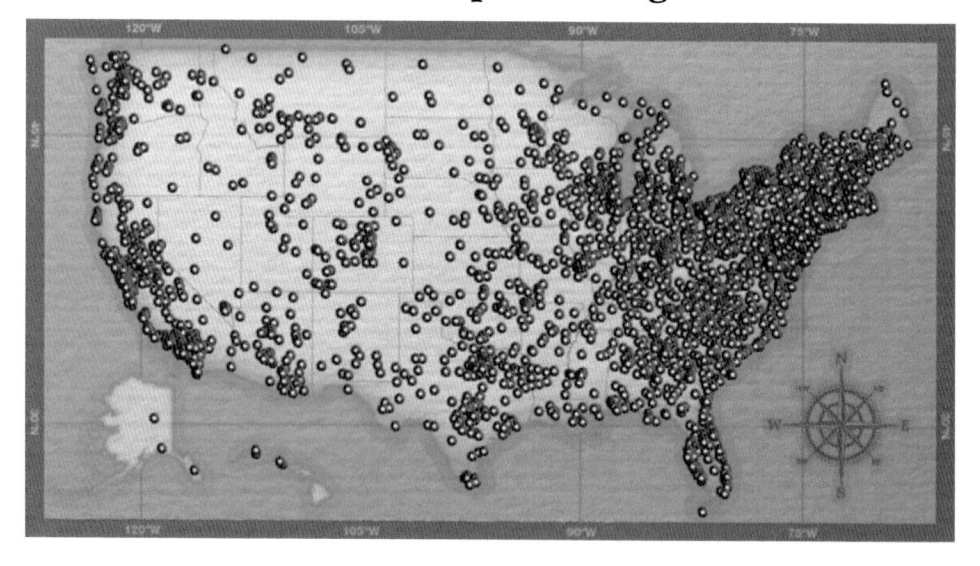

Search for your hometown history, your old stomping grounds, and even your favorite sports team.

Consistent with our mission to preserve history on a local level, this book was printed in South Carolina on American-made paper and manufactured entirely in the United States. Products carrying the accredited Forest Stewardship Council (FSC) label are printed on 100 percent FSC-certified paper.

MADE IN THE USA